Dangers of Artificial Intelligence

CHRISTA KELLY

childsworld.com

Published by The Child's World®
800-599-READ • www.childsworld.com

Photography Credits
Photographs ©: Olena Yakobchuk/Shutterstock Images, cover (man and robot), 1 (man and robot); Shutterstock Images, cover (background), 1 (background), 9, 13; NASA, 5; Henry Burroughs/AP Images, 6; Tada Images/Shutterstock Images, 11; Julie Star/Shutterstock Images, 14; Senior Airman Jessica Sanchez-Chen/US Air Force/DVIDS, 17; Kateryna Kon/Shutterstock Images, 18; Red Line Editorial, 21; Design elements from Tatiana Shepeleva/Shutterstock Images and Shutterstock Images

ISBN Information
9781503893795 (Reinforced Library Binding)
9781503894617 (Portable Document Format)
9781503895430 (Online Multi-user eBook)
9781503896253 (Electronic Publication)

LCCN 2024941386

Printed in the United States of America

ABOUT THE AUTHOR

Christa Kelly is an author and editor from Minnesota. She lives with her wife, Clare, and their two cats, Casey and Honey Cheddar.

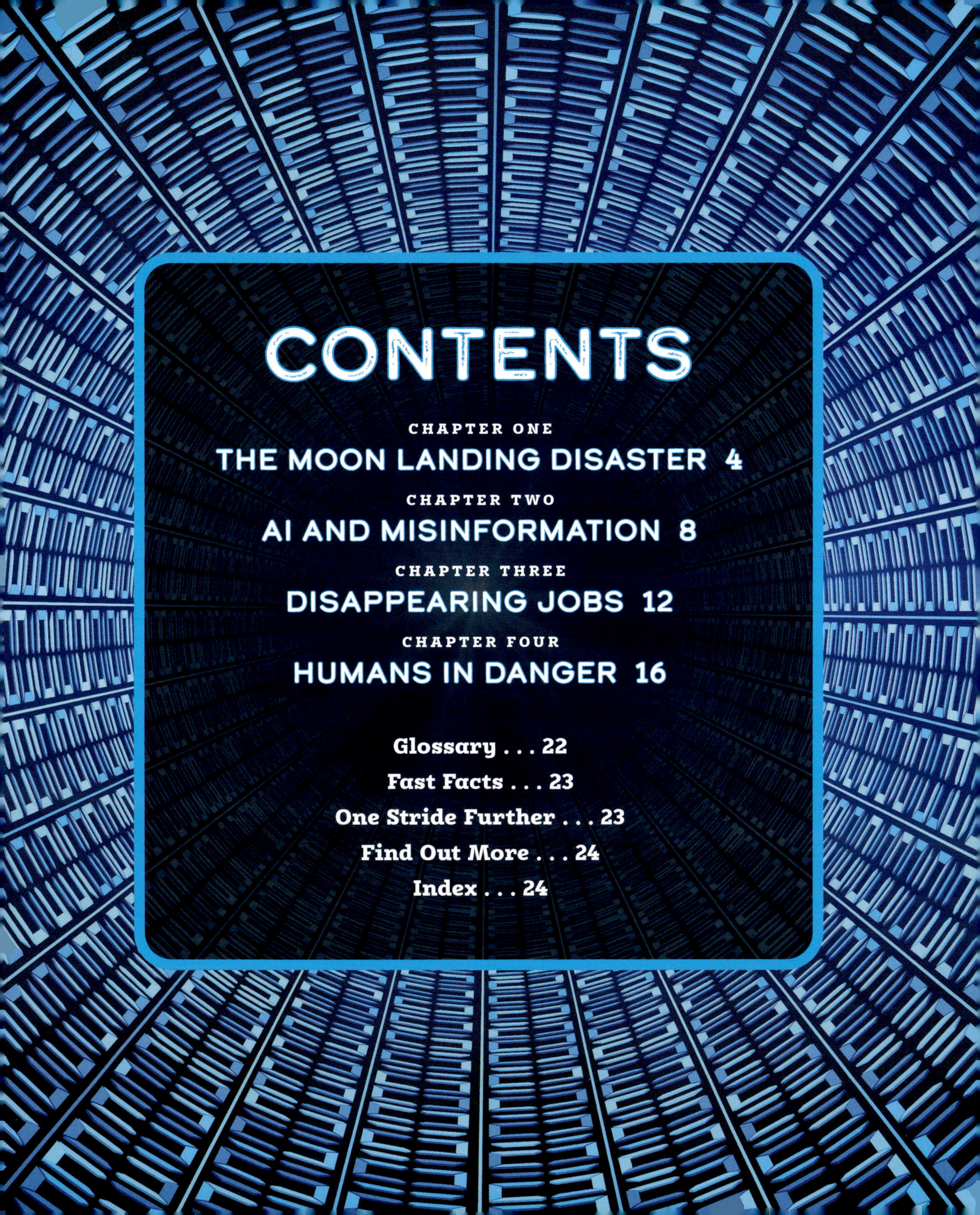

CONTENTS

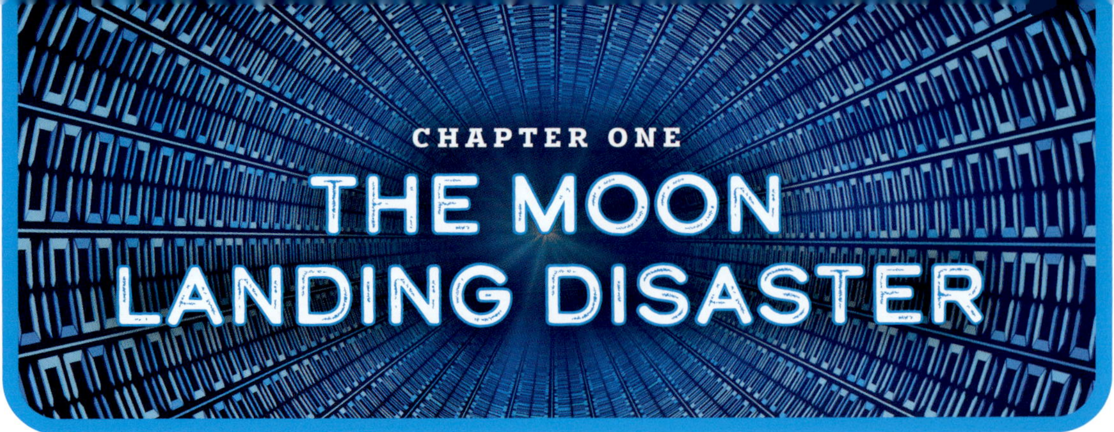

CHAPTER ONE

THE MOON LANDING DISASTER

It was July 1969. People around the world were watching the news on their televisions. Astronauts were about to land on the moon.

Suddenly, an alarm blared from the spaceship. Something had gone wrong. The video cut off. For a second, there was silence. Then the news cut to a speech from President Richard Nixon. He looked devastated.

Nixon told viewers that the mission to the moon had failed. The astronauts would never come home. They would be mourned as heroes.

The video of the disaster seemed real. The man speaking sounded like Nixon. He looked like Nixon, too. The video even used real footage from the moon landing. But it was not made in 1969. It was made in 2019 by two college students using artificial intelligence (AI). The students made it seem as if the moon landing had ended tragically. But in reality, the mission had been a success.

A Saturn V rocket carrying three astronauts launched into space toward the moon in 1969. It took the astronauts more than 3 days to reach the Moon from Earth.

AI studied real videos of Nixon speaking to create a deepfake of the former president.

The students used computers to make a realistic video of Nixon. They made him say things he had never actually said. This kind of video is known as a deepfake. Deepfakes are just one of the many things that AI allows people to do.

AI is an area of computer science. People working in AI write **programs** that can do tasks normally done only by humans. These tasks include **analyzing** large amounts of **data**, creating videos, and writing.

AI has quickly grown more powerful. It has also become widely used. It is found in cars and apps. It helps doctors and lawyers do their jobs. People can use AI to do a lot of good. But people can use AI to do bad things, too. People can use AI to spread false information. Workers can lose their jobs to AI. And some people worry that people could use AI for war or **terrorism**.

Some of these concerns could be addressed by new laws. But AI is developing very quickly. Lawmakers are having a hard time keeping up. As the power of AI grows, the possible dangers grow, too. Experts disagree about how big the risks are. Some think AI's benefits outweigh its dangers. However, others believe it could have devastating effects. Some think AI may even endanger the human race.

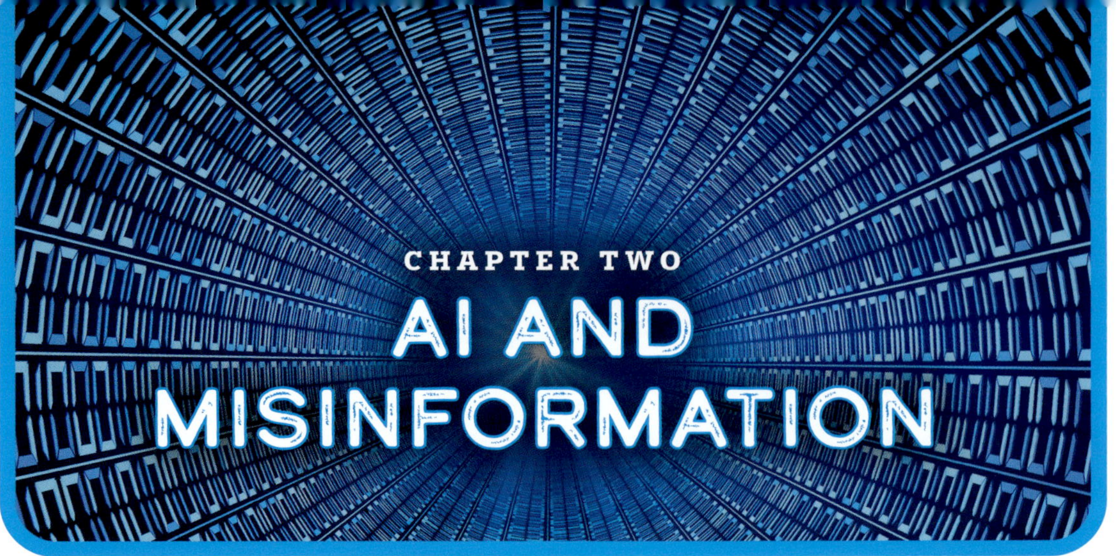

In 2022, a company called OpenAI released a program called ChatGPT. ChatGPT is an AI chatbot. People type messages to chatbots. Then the chatbots respond. They mimic human conversation. Chatbots can answer questions, keep people company, and even write stories.

In less than a week, ChatGPT had more than one million users. Users were amazed by what the program could do. Many trusted the information that ChatGPT provided. But the technology was often wrong.

ChatGPT is a large language model (LLM). LLMs are programs that collect and analyze massive amounts of text. This helps the programs learn what human language sounds like. When ChatGPT receives a message, it first uses complex **algorithms** to figure out what the user is saying. Then it uses its LLM training to figure out what words should make up its answer.

OpenAI gives ChatGPT text from a variety of sources, including books and websites.

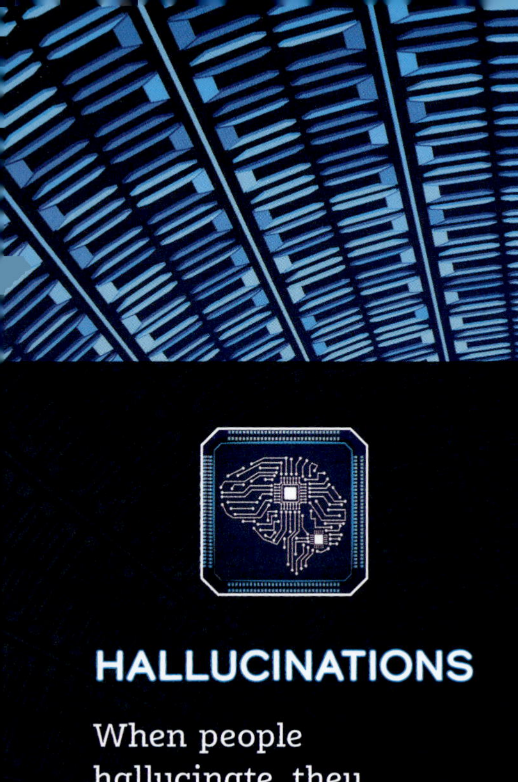

HALLUCINATIONS

When people hallucinate, they experience things that are not there. AI programs can hallucinate, too. Sometimes AI programs generate incorrect information. Other times, their answers do not seem to make sense at all. When these things happen, the AI is said to hallucinate. This can happen when the AI is trained incorrectly.

However, a 2024 study found that more than half of ChatGPT's answers contained incorrect information. This is because LLMs are trained using text that humans write. ChatGPT absorbs the mistakes people make in their writing. The program does not know when information is wrong, so it sometimes uses incorrect data in its answers. This leads the program to communicate false information.

Human mistakes are not the only bad information absorbed by AI. AI also absorbs human **biases**. Some people write hateful things on the internet. ChatGPT does not know that these messages are wrong. ChatGPT then absorbs these biases. They cause ChatGPT to create hateful content, such as racist messages.

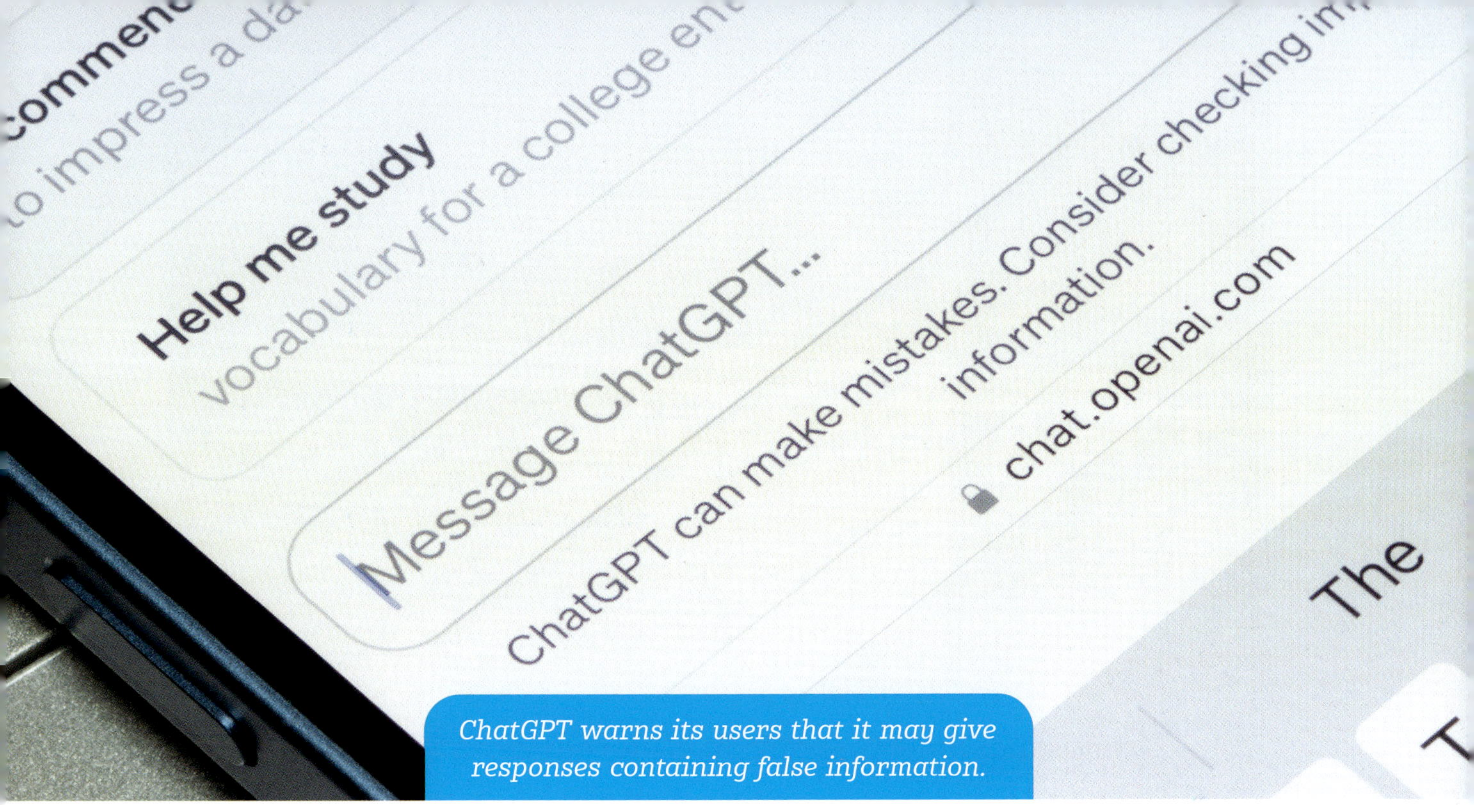

ChatGPT warns its users that it may give responses containing false information.

Other types of AI can unintentionally act in biased ways, too. The online shopping company Amazon tried using AI in hiring. The company trained an AI by showing it **résumés** of people hired by Amazon in the past. This helped the AI learn what type of candidates the company wanted. Then the company asked the AI to sort through new résumés. However, the hiring team soon found that the AI was biased. It preferred male candidates. The team realized this was because Amazon hired more men than people of other genders. The AI had decided that Amazon preferred male employees. It was reflecting the hiring team's bias.

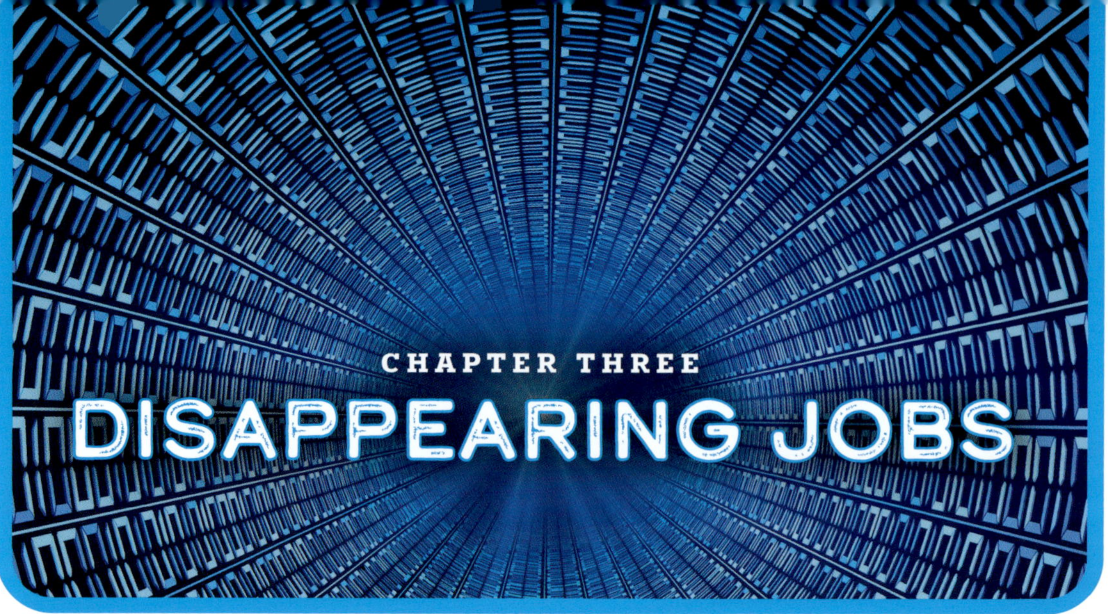

CHAPTER THREE

DISAPPEARING JOBS

Companies and workers are increasingly using AI to do tasks. This can make work easier. But it can also cause people to lose their jobs.

AI has many advantages over human workers. Computers do not need to be paid. They do not need breaks. And they can make fewer mistakes than humans. This makes them desirable workers for businesses.

AI has caused some people to lose their jobs. In 2023, a survey found that more than one-third of companies using AI reported replacing human workers with AI. More than 40 percent expected to replace more workers in 2024.

The invention of new technology has replaced jobs in the past. AI has the potential to replace even more jobs in the future.

One company produces delivery robots that use AI to carry items to people.

People with repetitive jobs are at the highest risk of being replaced by AI technology. **Manufacturing** is an area with many of these jobs. Companies are beginning to use robots powered by AI. These robots are able to do tasks formerly done by human workers. For example, the car company BMW uses AI-powered robots in one of its factories to check cars for mistakes. Using AI helps businesses make more money. But it can also take jobs away from human workers.

Customer service is another area that is changing due to AI. Many employees in this field are being replaced by chatbots. Chatbots can schedule appointments for customers. They can help people manage their insurance. They can even take fast-food orders. This technology could replace human customer service workers around the world.

Though AI is taking many jobs, experts predict it will create jobs, too. AI requires lots of data. New jobs will involve collecting and preparing data for AI. Companies will need to hire people to train AI programs. They will also need people to make sure AI programs work correctly.

AI AND ARTISTS

Some AI programs create images. Users can ask these programs to make new images. They can also ask the AI to make art in a variety of styles. These AI programs are trained on work made by human artists. These artists are sometimes paid for the use of their art. But others have their art used by AI without their permission. This has upset many artists.

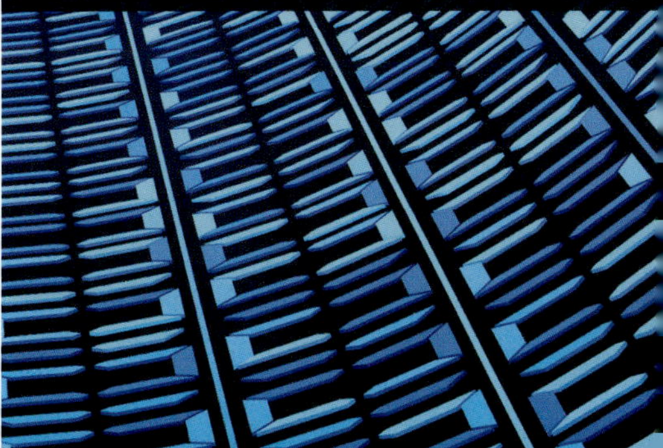

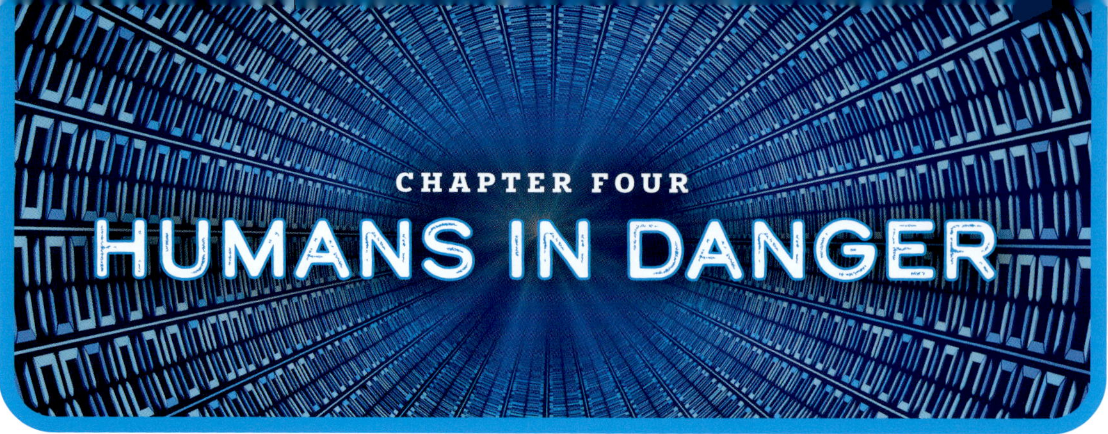

CHAPTER FOUR

HUMANS IN DANGER

AI is a powerful tool. People can use it for good. But people can also use it to hurt others. For example, people use AI in war. Militaries use AI to analyze **satellite images**. This helps armies understand what is happening on the battlefield. Soldiers are then able to make decisions and target enemies more quickly.

AI can be used in other ways, too. Militaries are researching AI-controlled weapons. These weapons would use sensors to find and destroy targets on their own. Sensors are devices that detect information from the real world, such as light or heat. AI-controlled weapons could take the form of **drones** or missiles.

Experts warn that AI-controlled weapons could be incredibly dangerous. Without human control, these weapons could harm or kill innocent people. Some AI-controlled weapons already exist. But as AI technology improves, these tools could become much deadlier.

This drone was developed by the US Air Force. It uses AI to navigate its surroundings and track targets. A human controller can choose to fire the drone's net gun, which releases a net that can take down other drones.

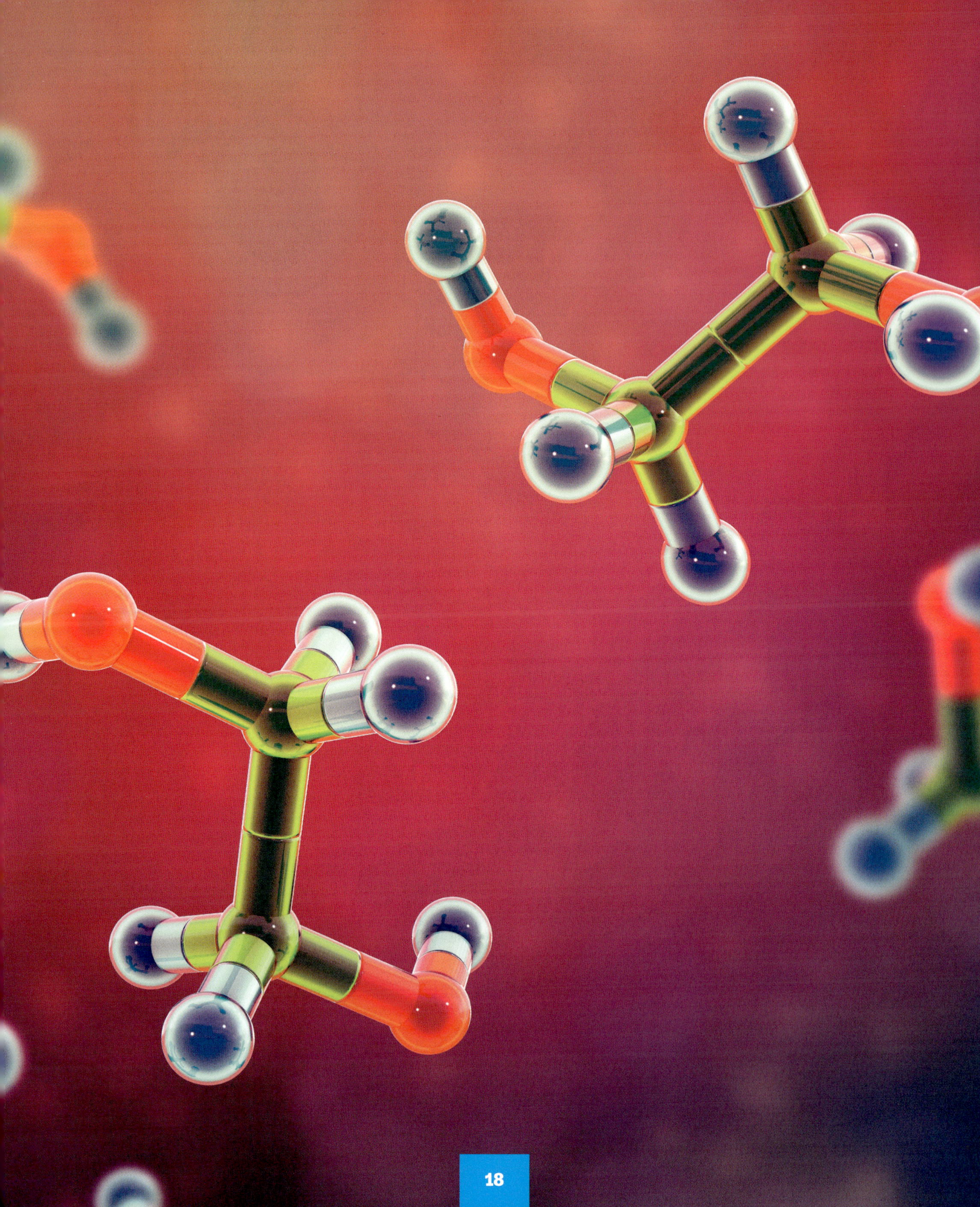

Experts also worry that AI could be used to create biological weapons. Biological weapons use diseases or poisonous materials to harm people. People have used these weapons in war for more than a thousand years. But AI could make it easier than ever to create these weapons. Scientists can use AI to create new medicines. However, this same technology could be used to make deadly poisons. In 2022, researchers used a medical AI program to invent chemicals that could be used as weapons. In just 6 hours, the program invented 40,000 new deadly chemical compounds.

AI also has negative effects on the environment. This is because AI requires a lot of electricity. Much of the electricity people use comes from burning substances such as coal, natural gas, and oil. When these substances are burned, they release gases into the air. These gases raise Earth's temperature, harming the environment. By 2027, AI could use as much energy as a small country.

Chemical compounds are made of molecules, which are composed of smaller parts called atoms. AI can study the structure of chemical compounds to create new ones.

Some experts worry that AI could grow too intelligent. It could then decide to destroy its creators. Geoffrey Hinton is a computer scientist. He spent his career improving AI. But he later claimed that AI was getting too powerful. He urged scientists to find ways to prevent AI from taking over. However, many experts believe this concern is unnecessary. They say the odds of the technology destroying humanity are low.

AI can spread misinformation. It can replace people in the workforce. It can even be used to kill people. But although AI can be used for harm, it can also be used for good. People must learn how to use the technology wisely. For better or for worse, AI is here to stay.

COULD AI DESTROY HUMANITY?

AI may someday advance to the point of being able to perform all human tasks. Researchers asked 2,704 AI experts how likely they thought it was that AI would cause an extremely bad event such as human extinction if it advanced to that level.

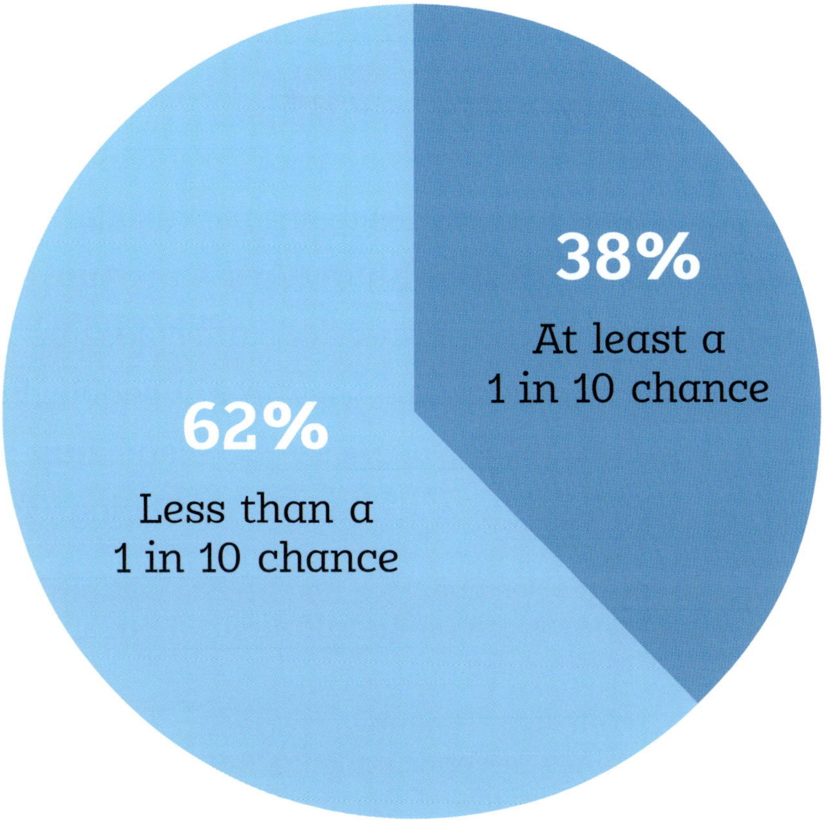

38%

At least a 1 in 10 chance

62%

Less than a 1 in 10 chance

A 2023 survey of AI experts found that most believed it was unlikely that AI would lead to human extinction, even if AI advanced to the point of being able to perform all human tasks.

GLOSSARY

algorithms (AL-guh-rih-thumz) Algorithms are step-by-step instructions used to solve a problem or perform a task. Some AI programs use algorithms to create text and images.

analyzing (AN-uh-lye-zing) A person or AI program is analyzing something if it is studying it in detail. ChatGPT can tell what a user is asking by analyzing the user's messages.

biases (BYE-uss-iz) Biases are unfair opinions for or against someone or something. AI programs reflect the biases of the people who design them and of the data they are given.

data (DAY-tuh) Data is information collected for a purpose. People train chatbots with massive amounts of data.

drones (DROHNZ) Drones are vehicles that fly but do not carry people. The military uses drones to attack enemy targets.

manufacturing (man-yoo-FAK-chur-ing) Manufacturing is the creation of products from raw materials. Some manufacturing companies use AI in their factories.

programs (PROH-gramz) Programs are sets of instructions that tell a computer how to do tasks. Chatbots are programs that can use AI to communicate with people.

résumés (REH-zuh-mayz) Résumés are documents containing information about people's working backgrounds. Amazon trained an AI using a biased set of résumés.

satellite images (SA-tuh-lyte IH-muh-jiz) Satellite images are photos of Earth taken by machines in space called satellites. Militaries can use AI to analyze satellite images of battlefields.

terrorism (TAYR-ur-iz-um) Terrorism is the political use of violence against innocent people. AI could be used to commit acts of terrorism.

FAST FACTS

- AI is an area of computer science that involves writing programs that can do tasks normally done only by humans.
- Chatbots are programs that use AI to communicate with users.
- Chatbots are trained on data that contains human errors. This causes chatbots to sometimes produce misinformation.
- Human workers in fields such as manufacturing and customer service may be replaced by AI.
- Though AI has replaced some human employees, it has also created jobs.
- People can use AI to control weapons and create dangerous chemical compounds.
- Some people worry that AI could destroy humanity, but many experts say this is unlikely.

ONE STRIDE FURTHER

- What are some additional ways AI could be dangerous?
- What are some jobs you think AI could not do better than human workers?
- Do you believe the benefits of AI outweigh the dangers? Why or why not?

FIND OUT MORE

IN THE LIBRARY

Kulz, George Anthony. *Generative Artificial Intelligence.* Parker, CO: The Child's World, 2025.

Williams, Dinah. *Artificial Intelligence.* New York, NY: Starry Forest Books, 2021.

Williams, Haley. *Jobs and Artificial Intelligence.* Parker, CO: The Child's World, 2025.

ON THE WEB

Visit our website for links about the dangers of artificial intelligence:
childsworld.com/links

Note to Parents, Caregivers, Teachers, and Librarians: We routinely verify our web links to make sure they are safe and active sites. So encourage your readers to check them out!

INDEX